Ice Cream C...

25 Low Carb – Low Sugar Ice Cream Recipes

Recipe Collection by: Cora Pepper

Copyright 2017 Speckled Egg Publishing. All rights reserved. The material in this book my not be reproduced without permission. The Ice Cream Cookbook, and written works by Cora Pepper is solely owned by Speckled Egg Publishing.

Printed in the United States of America

Recipes are not intended to be any type of medical advice. If you have special diatary needs for a health condition you should consult a nutritional specialist for your meal planning.

Table of Contents

Dieter's Delight

Chapter 1 – The Quickest and Easiest Ice Cream Recipes (Recipes 1 – 9)

Chapter 2 – Variations of Favorite Pumpkin Ice Creams (Recipes 10 – 13)

Chapter 3 – Low Carb Chocolate Ice Cream Deserts (Recipes 14 – 17)

Chapter 4 – Most Popular Flavors of Keto Frozen Treats (Recipes 18 – 25)

Additional Notes About Recipes

Free Bonus Recipes (Recipes 25 – 30)

Dieter's Delight

Dieters, suffer no more! Fad diets come and go, but they all have one thing in common these days. They cut significantly back on sugar. So, no matter which technique you try to tackle when putting your weekly meals together, you are going to want to include sweets and cheats that cut back on the sugar intake. If you're like me, ice creams are your favorite sweet treat and a vulnerability when it comes to keeping true to your diet goals.

Now you can incorporate these ice cream recipes into just about any diet style. We have specifically designed low carb, low sugar ice cream recipes so that you can enjoy your favorite dessert while you enjoy a successful nutritional lifestyle.

Not only are our recipes healthy, they are made with good fats. You won't want to buy ice creams that are loaded with sugar from the super market ever again after choosing your favorite flavors out of this book. Good luck and Happy ice cream making!

Chapter 1
The Quickest & Easiest Ice Cream Recipes

The quickest and easiest ice cream recipes in this book are made with instant ice cream techniques. You do not need an ice cream maker or any kind of specialty machine to make these recipes. Each recipe can be made with regular ingredients or with a low carb, ketogenic sugar substitute. In this section, each recipe will give you both options. The option you choose will depend on your preference for flavor or dietary needs. Please read the recipes carefully, so that you don't add both choices to each dish you prepare.

Some of the instant frozen treats in this chapter are not "true" ice creams, but they are fast and easy, and will make a frozen ice cream like treat that you will tweak to your flavor with a little practice. These are combinations of ice cream recipes, frozen yogurt, sorbets, and sherbet. All can be low-carb ketogentic treats.

The following recipes can be made in a baking dish or bread loaf dish and rolled out with a spoon or ice cream scooper for a terrific serving.

Recipes 1 – 9

1. Simple Blackberry Delight
2. Simplest Home-Made Vanilla
3. Pineapple Coconut Yogurt
4. Lemon Yogurt Freezy Treat
5. Simplest Strawberry
6. No Cook Blueberry Cheese Cake Ice Cream
7. Almond Keto Frozen Yogurt
8. Frozen Banana Delight
9. Low Carb Mocha Ice Cream Bar

1. You will need:

- 1 cup of fresh black berries
- 2 cups of frozen yogurt
- 2 tsps. of Truvia (or 3 tbps. of sugar)
- 1 disposable plastic storage container with lid

1. Information:

Prep time: 2 minutes

Total time: 45 minutes

Serves: 6 (1/2 cup)

Calories per serving: 170

Total Calories: 1,020

Carbohydrates: 28

Information is based on regular plain yogurt. Your calories and carbs will vary slightly if you choose to substitute fat free or low-fat types. Make sure to read the container and adjust based on the product you buy.

1: Simple Blackberry Delight

The simplest ice cream treats are ice cream-like in flavor and texture without the prep time and effort that goes into making true ice cream. This frozen yogurt treat is a much healthier choice for those who have a sweet tooth.

First, place the blackberries and plain yogurt into a blender and mix until completely blended. Add 2 tsps. of Truvia. Truvia is our preferred sugar substitute due to it being as close to the most natural form of sugar. You can subsititue Splend or sugar if you are not concerned about calories.

Taste the yogurt and add enough sweeterner to your liking. Scoop the mixture into the disposable sealable container. Cover with its lid and allow this to set in the freezer for 40-40 minutes. Serve when it is Scoopable and rolls smoothly into balls with your spoon.

2. You will need:

- 1 cup of heavy cream
- 2 tsp. of vanilla extract
- 2 tsps. of Truvia (or 3 tbsps. of sugar)
- 2 plastic cooking bags
- 1 pinch of salt
- 2 cups of ice cubes
- 1 tpsp. Of sea salt
- 1 towel

2. Information:

Prep time: 5 minutes

Total time: 15 minutes.

Serves: 2 - 3 (1/2 cup)

Calories per serving: 400 - 450

Total Calories: 800 - 1000

Carbohydrates: 3.5 g.

Information is based on heavy cream. Your calories and carbs will vary slightly if you choose to substitute other types of cream. Make sure to read the container and adjust based on the product you buy.

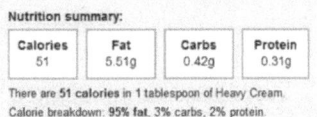

2. Simplest Home-Made Vanilla

This vanilla ice cream recipe is the easiest way to make a true ice cream with the minimal tools possible. No ice cream making machine required. Using heavy cream is high in calories, but very low in carbs. This is truly a low carb treat, but remember moderation is necessary because of the number of calories. Cream is a low carb dieter's friend, but keep reasonable perspective on how you use it.

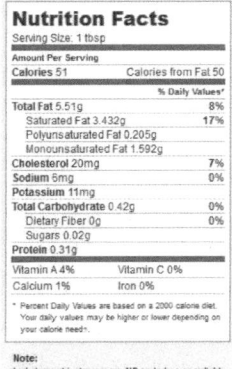

First, fill one plastic bag with ice cubes and salt. In the second bad add the cream, vanilla extract, and Truvia. Tie the second bag closed and place it inside the first bag with the ice cubes. Make sure the bag with the cream is completely covered in ice. Add more ice cubes if needed. Wrap the entire bag with a towel, and shake. The ice ceam will begin to form. The time it takes varies for every batch when it is made this way. After the ice cream is formed, open the bag and serve in a dish.

3. You will need:

- 2 cups of plain yogurt
- 1 cup of fresh chopped pineapple
- 2 tsps. of Truvia (or 3 tsps. of sugar)
- ½ tbsp. of lemon juice
- 2 tbsps. of fresh coconut shavings
- 1 disposable plastic storage container with lid

3. Information:

Prep time: 5 minutes

Total time: 30 minutes

Serves: 6 (1/2 cup)

Calories per serving: 140

Total Calories: 840

Carbohydrates: 24

Information is based on regular plain yogurt. Your calories and carbs will vary slightly if you choose to substitute fat free or low-fat types. Make sure to read the container and adjust based on the product you buy.

3: Pineapple Coconut Yogurt

To make sure you get an accurate calorie and carb count be sure to use freshly cut fruit. You can make this easily with canned fruit, but the sugar saturated syrup will change the calorie and carb count, as well as affect the freshness of your final product.

Add the frozen pineapple, Truvia, yogurt & lemon juice into a blender. Mix this until smooth and fully blended. Blend for a full 2 minutes. Fold the coconut shaving into the mixture.

Spoon this into your feezable disposable storage container and seal with a lid. Freeze for upto 6 hours for a solid product, or less if you want a soft serve version.

Note: Remember coconut shavings come in 2 types plain and sugar coated. The sugar coated are sweet and delicious, but if you are sugar conscious opt for the plain coconut shavings. They are still so yummy.

4. You will need:

- ½ cup of heavy cream
- 1 cup of plain yogurt
- 1 tbsp. of lemon juice
- ¼ tsp. of vanilla extract
- 2 tsps. of Truvia (or 3 tsps. of sugar)
- 2 plastic cooking bags
- 1 tsp. of salt
- A towel
- Ice cubes

4. Information:

Prep time: 10 minutes

Total time: 45 minutes

Serves: 2 (1/2 cup)

Calories per serving: 310

Total Calories: 620

Carbohydrates: 20 g.

Information is based on regular plain yogurt. Your calories and carbs will vary slightly if you choose to substitute fat free or low-fat types. Make sure to read the container and adjust based on the product you buy.

4: Lemon Yogurt Freezy Treat

Lemon frozen yogurt is a popular choice for a summertime dessert. You can modify this recipe with any of your favorite citris flavors. Orange, grapefruit, and lime can be exchanged for lemon or blended to your preference. Citric fruits are full of vitamin C and folic acid, excellent for a well balanced healthy diet.

This is the simplest way to make ice cream without the need for a machine. Put the salt and ice cubes in one bag. Fill the second bag with the cream, yogurt, vanilla, Truvia, and lemon juice. Seal the bag tightly and place it inside the bag with the icecubes. Seal this tightly. Wrap it in a towel and shake the bag for 10 minutes. Open and serve.

Note: if you want your citrus flavor to be a little stronger shave a little bit of zest from the lemon or orange. You only need a tiny sprinkle for a powerful flavor. Most people prefer the lighter taste with just the juice.

5. You will need:

- 1 cup of heavy cream
- 1 tsp. of vanilla extract
- 1 cup of cut strawberries
- 1 drop of pink coloring
- 2 tsps. of Truvia (or 3 tbsps. of sugar)
- 2 plastic cooking bags
- 1 pinch of salt
- 2 cups of ice cubes
- 1 tpsp. Of sea salt
- 1 towel

5. Information:

Prep time: 5 minutes

Total time: 30 minutes.

Serves: 4 (1/2 cup)

Calories per serving: 400 - 450

Total Calories: 800 - 1000

Carbohydrates: 9 g.

Information is based on heavy cream. Your calories and carbs will vary slightly if you choose to substitute other types of cream. Make sure to read the container and adjust based on the product you buy.

5: Simplest Strawberry

This strawberry ice cream recipe is the easiest way to make a true ice cream with the minimal tools possible. Using heavy cream is high in calories, but very low in carbs. Strawberry is a delightful and popular flavor also very low in carbs, but remember you can exchange them for any berry flavor of your choice. Do you want to get a soft serve look to your home-made serving? See below.

First, blend the heavy cream, strawberries, vanilla extract, and Truvia in a blender until thoroughly blended. Drop one drop of pink coloring and bled for 1 – 2 minutes. Fill one plastic bag with ice cubes and salt. In the second bag add the mixture from the blender. Tie the second bag closed and place it inside the first bag with the ice cubes. Make sure the bag with the cream is completely covered in ice. Add more ice cubes if needed. Wrap the entire bag with a towel, and shake. The ice ceam will begin to form. The time it takes varies for every batch when it is made this way. After the ice cream is formed, open the bag and serve in a dish.

Note: If you want to get a textured soft serve look for your guests make the recipe in a large cakemakers frosting bag. Cut the tip and place a large star tip at the bottom. Twist the end while you are making the ice cream and secure with an elastic. Once the ice cream is ready to serve snip the elastic and pipe it into the dish like frosting.

Just as in frosting making, this may take a little practice. If your finished product is too soft you can set it in the freezer to thicken quicker.

_____

6. You will need:

- 1 and 1/4 cup of Truvia
- 1 package of cream cheese
- 4 large egg yolks
- 3 cups of 2% milk
- 1 cup of half and half
- 3 cups of fresh blueberries
- ¼ cup of water
- 2 plastic cooking bags
- 2 tbsp of salt
- ice cubes
- a towel

6. Information:

Prep time: 2 minutes

Total time: 45 minutes

Serves: 6 (1/2 cup)

Calories per serving: 170

Total Calories: 1,020

Carbohydrates: 28

Information is based on regular plain yogurt. Your calories and carbs will vary slightly if you choose to substitute fat free or low-fat types. Make sure to read the container and adjust based on the product you buy.

6: No Cook Blueberry Cheese Cake Ice Cream

Do you love a summer treat of blueberries and cream? We have our own low carb version in a blueberry cheese cake icecream.

Combine the egg yolks, sour cream, and 1 cup of Truvia in a large bowl with a beater. Combine the milk and half and half in a second bowl. Whisk half of the milk mixture to the cheese mixture while stirring constantly. Put the remaining half of the milk in the fridge.

Combine blueberries, ¼ cup of Truvia, and ¼ cup of water into the blender. Blend for one minute. Add the cheese mixture and blend for 1 minute.

Pour this mixture into a large plastic cooking bag and tie the top. Place this bag into a second bag filled with ice cubes and 2 tbsps. of salt. Wrap it in a towel and set this in the freezer for 1-3 hours. Continue checking until the ice cream is done.

7. You will need:

- 2 cups non-fat plain yogurt
- 1 cups of vanilla soy milk
- 3 tsps. of Truvia
- ¼ cup of finely chopped almonds
- 1 disposable plastic storage container with lid

7. Information:

Prep time: 10 minutes

Total time: 35 minutes

Serves: 6 (1/2 cup)

Calories per serving: 70

Total Calories: 400

Carbohydrates: 19

Information is based on plain nonfat yogurt. Your calories and carbs will vary slightly if you choose to substitute other types. Make sure to read the container and adjust based on the product you buy.

7: Almond Keto Frozen Yogurt

If you are shooting for flavor packed into few calories and low carbs. This almond frozen yogurt recipe is so sweet and delicious. If you love the creamy taste of vanilla soy milk, this is the frozen treat for you.

Blend the ingrediants well in a mixer for 1 – 3 minutes. If you have an ice cream machine, pour it into the machine and churn for 30 minutes. If you are without a machine pour the mixture into a large cooking bag. Fill a second cooking bag with 1 table spoon of salt and 2 cups of ice cubes. Place the sealed mixture into the bag with ice. Cover the mixture with 2 more cups of ice cubes and tie it at the top. Wrap a towel around the bag and place it in the freezer for 1 – 3 hours. Serve when ready.

8. You will need:

- 4 sliced bananas
- 2 cups of vanilla yogurt
- 1/4 cup of finely chopped marichino cherries
- 2 tsps. of Truvia (or 4 tsps. of sugar)
- 1 disposable plastic storage container with lid

8. Information:

Prep time: 5 minutes

Total time: 45 minutes

Serves: 8 (1/2 cup)

Calories per serving: 100

Total Calories: 800

Carbohydrates: 19

Information is based on regular plain yogurt. Your calories and carbs will vary slightly if you choose to substitute fat free or low-fat types. Make sure to read the container and adjust based on the product you buy.

8: Frozen Banana Delight

This is a healthy kid friendly frozen yogurt treat with a touch of candy like color that make the kids eyes pop with happiness.

Put all the ingredients into a blender and blend for 1-2 ful minutes. If you want your red cherries to come out in small speckles add the cherries to the blender. If you want larger pieces for a brighter color contrast quarter the pieces by hand and mix them into the bananas and yogurt after they have been blended.

Churn in your icecream maker for 30 minutes and freez in a sealable container.

If you do not have an ice cream maker use the double bag method as described in the recipes listed above.

9. You will need:

- 3 cups of coconut milk
- 2 tsp. of Knox gelatin
- 6 tsps. of Truvia
- 2 tbsps. of cocoa powder
- 3 egg yolks
- ½ tsp. vanilla extract
- 2 oz. of sugar free chocolate shell
- Freezer pop container
- Wooden sticks

9. Information:

Prep time: 15 minutes

Total time: 1 -3 hours

Serves: 6 (1/2 cup)

Calories per serving: 300

Total Calories: 1,800

Carbohydrates: 11

Information is based on regular plain yogurt. Your calories and carbs will vary slightly if you choose to substitute fat free or low-fat types. Make sure to read the container and adjust based on the product you buy.

9: Low Carb Mocha Ice Ceam Bar

Coconut milk is an amazing substitute in treats that are mocha, chocolate, or coffee flavored. Coconut milk has a rich creamy texture. This recipe is naturally low in carbs.

In a saucepan combine ½ of the coconut milk and the Knox. Heat and stir until dissolved. Then add the remaining coconut milk, sweetner, and cocoa powder.

In a separate bowl combine the egg yolk, vanilla, and remaining coconut milk. Add this to the sauce pan. Stir for 3 minutes, and remove from the heat.

Once cooled down, pour the mixture into the popsicle molds. Add wooden sticks, and freeze for 1 hour.

Finally, remove from the mold and drizzle the chocolate shell over the bars until solid.

Chapter 2
Variations of Favorite Pumpkin Ice Creams

When the autumn arrives and the Holiday season is about to begin cafes, and treat shops are burstin with pumpkin flavored products. Business studies show that the number one most popular seasonal flavors are pumpkin, pumpkin spice, pumpkin pie. We can't leave pumplkin ice creamoff the menu. Here are a few variations of our favorite pumpkim recipes that will be loved when you make your first batch in October and serve right up to your New Years celebration party.

Note: If you are carb and sugar conscious our pumpkin recipes might be especially attractive. Although regular ice cream is high in sugar and calories naturally, the flavors that are made at specialty stores in the form of frozen drinks are jam packed with more sugar than you would reasonably consume on a normal diet. In some cases, there is an entire cup of sugar in a large frozen treat in the form of syrup, candy, and raw sugar. These recipes are far more health friendly.

Recipes (10 – 13)

10. Simplest Pumpkin Frozen Treat
11. Pumpkin Spice Ice Cream
12. Pumpkin Pie Ice Cream
13. Banana Pumpkin Rich Desert

10. Simplest Pumpkin Frozen Treat

10. You will need:

- 1 cup of fat free milk
- 2 tbsp. of cream
- 2 tsps. of Truvia
- 1 banana
- ½ tsp. of vanilla extract
- 1/2 cup of pumpkin puree
- ¼ tsp. of pumpkin pie spice
- 1 disposable plastic storage container with lid

10. Information:

Prep time: 20 minutes

Total time: 1 hour

Serves: 4 (1/2 cup)

Calories per serving: 150

Total Calories: 600

Carbohydrates: 17

In a blender mix all the ingredients together. If you are using an ice cream machine, spoon this into the machine and churn for 30 minutes. Remove from the machine and serve, or place it in a sealable container and freeze.

If you do not have an ice cream machine, you will need to use the plastic bag method. Place the mixture in one plastic cooking bag and close tightly. Fill a second bag half way with ice. Place the first bag inside the second bag with the ice. Cover with more ice, add ½ tbsp. of salt and seal. Wrap this in a towel for insulation. Place in the freezer for 20 minutes, and check on it until it is done. Serve when the ice cream is at the thickness and consistency that you like.

11. You will need:

- 1 cup of pumpkin puree
- 4 eggs
- 4 egg yolks
- 2 tsps. of Truvia
- 1/3 cup of food grade cocoa butter
- 1/3 cup of food grade coconut oil
- ½ cup of ice
- 1 disposable plastic storage container with lid

11. Information:

Prep time: 10 minutes

Total time: Immediately

Serves: 6 (1/2 cup)

Calories per serving: 200

Total Calories: 1,200

Carbohydrates: 12

Note about ingredients: make sure your oils are food grade. You can buy cocoa butter and coconut oil for DIY projects that are not for cooking, and many people find these products online if they aren't on your local store shelves.

11. Pumpkin Spice Ice Cream

Pumpkin spice is often the flavor that people recognize when they order a pumpkin product at their favorite café. You can make your version at home.

Blend all the ingredients into a mixture in the blender for 1 minute. Scoop into a sealable container and freez for one hour. Scoop and serve.

This recipe is not a true ice cream, and doesn't need to be churned. You can freeze it into an ice cream like freezy treat, or you can add more ice and turn it into a freezy slush drink.

12. You will need:

- 1 cup of whole milk
- ½ cup of Truvia (or ¾ cup of sugar)
- 1 cup of pumpkin puree
- 1 tsp. of pumpkin pie spice
- 2 cups of heavy cream
- Ghram cracker crumbs
- 1 disposable plastic storage container with lid

12. Information:

Prep time: 10 minutes

Total time: 20 minutes

Serves: 12 (1/2 cup)

Calories per serving: 300

Total Calories: 4000

Carbohydrates: 17

Adjust the truvia amounts to your liking of sweetness.

12. Pumpkin Pie Ice Cream

In this version, we will replicate that Thanksgiving pumpkin pie desert. This is slightly different from pumpkin spice. Pumpkin pie flavors are sweeter and more of a cream and vanilla flavor.

In a pan on the stove top, bring the milk, sugar, pumpkin puree, pumpkin pie spice, and vanilla extract to a low simmer, stirring frequently.

Allow the mixture to cool slightly, then add heavy cream. Cover and refrigerate until well chilled.

Churn the mixture for 30 minutes in your ice cream machine. Scoop the ice cream into a sealable container. Freeze until firm. Serve with crushed graham cracker crumbs as a topping.

If you do not have an ice cream maching, use the double bag method for churning your ice cream as described in the recipe above.

13. Banana Pumpkin Rich Desert (Keto Recipe)

Banana is often used in frozen pumpkin treats as a healthy way to thicken the puree. It has a creamy flavor and often goes unnoticed, but if you use a generous amount you can taste the banana and discover how these two fruits compliment each other in a dessert dish.

Add everything into the blender except the bananas. Transfer them to a small dish or ice tray. Peel and freez the bananas separately. Once frozen place them back into the blender with the frozen bananas. This will give you a frozen treat ready to serve immediately. Place in the freezer when done.

13. You will need:

- 2 cups of pumpkin puree
- ¼ tsp. of pumpkin spice
- 2 tsps. of Truvia
- 1 tsp. of vanilla extract
- ½ cup of carrot juice
- 6 – 8 dates (optional)
- 5 – 6 medium size bananas
- 1 disposable plastic storage container with lid

13. Information:

Prep time: 10 minutes

Total time: 1 hour

Serves: 10 (1/2 cup)

Calories per serving: 220

Total Calories: 2200

Carbohydrates: 17

Chapter 3
Low Carb Chocolate Ice Cream Deserts

A study in Norway once concluded that chocolate cravings are a cultural trait. Women often crave chocolate in America, and entire businesses have been built around the idea that chocolate is something desired in relation to hormore fluctuation and a woman's need for the nutrients found in cocoa. It turns out, if you are one of those who must have chocolate on a rainy day, or a busy day, or to manage your stress, you probably learned it from your mother. Chocolate cravings are not specific to women. Men also crave chocolate too. We all know that this treat is as high in calories and sugar as it is high in demand.

Try a home-made version with sugar substitutes and variations. This way you can really enjoy your chocolate and be satisfied at the same time.

The following recipes can be made in a baking dish or bread loaf dish and rolled out with a spoon or ice cream scooper for a terrific serving.

Recipes (14 – 17)

14. Low Carb Hand Made Chocolate Ice Cream
15. Easy Chocolate Frozen Yogurt
16. Mint Chocolate Chip Ice Cream
17. Grandma's Chocolate Ice Cream

14. You will need:

- 2 cans of evaporated milk (12. oz cans)
- 1 cup of whole milk
- ½ cup. of Truvia (or 1 cup of sugar)
- 2/3 cup of Hersheys sugarfree chocolate syrup
- 2 large plastic cooking bags
- Ice cubes
- 2 tbsps. of salt

14. Information:

Prep time: 5 minutes

Total time: 1-2 hours

Serves: 8 (1/2 cup)

Calories per serving: 160

Total Calories: 1,264

Carbohydrates: 15

Like allf our recipes, you have the choise to replace raw sugar with a sugar substitute. The information provided above is calculated as a low sugar product. If you choose to use granulated sugar your carb and calorie count will increase.

14. Low Sugar – Low Carb Hand Made Chocolate Ice Cream

Chocolate is a die hard craving for some, but sugar free chocolate flavors are notorious for being bland and disappointing. Try using a familiar store brand like Hersheys when making sugar free chocolate. If the mixture seems bland increase the sugar substitute to your liking before freezing.

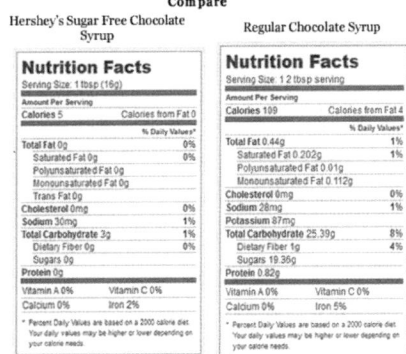

Note: The nutrition facts on the right are written for 2 table spoons of syrup, while the facts on the left are written for 1.

Mix all the ingredients in a large bowl and blend well. If you are using an ice cream maker pour the ingredients into your maker and freeze according to your ice cream makers instructions. (Times vary depending on manufacturer.) Remove the ice cream and place in an air tight sealable container and freeze for 6 hours.

If you do not have an ice cream maker place the mixture in a large cooking bag and seal. A turkey bag is a good size. Fll another cooking bag with ice and salt and place the first bag into the second. Tie this closed. Wrap it in a towel and allow it to turn into ice cream. Once it starts to thicken transfer it to a sealable container and freeze.

15. You will need:

- 1 cup of 2% milk
- 2 cups of frozen yogurt
- 3 tsps. of Truvia
- ½ cup of unsweetened cocoa powder
- 1 tsp. of vanilla extract
- 1 disposable plastic storage container with lid

15. Information:

Prep time: 2 minutes

Total time: 1 hour

Serves: 6 (1/2 cup)

Calories per serving: 130

Total Calories: 780

Carbohydrates: 14

Information is based on regular plain yogurt. Your calories and carbs will vary slightly if you choose to substitute fat free or low-fat types. Make sure to read the container and adjust based on the product you buy.

15. Easy Chocolate Frozen Yogurt

This is the easiest chocolate frozen yogurt recipe available. Even though the recipe is for frozen yogurt, you can churn this in your ice cream maker for 30 minutes to get the same smooth consistency you get in ice cream.

Blend all the ingredients in a blender for 1 minute and transfer into your disposable sealable plastic container.

Of course, you do not need to use your ice cream manchine, nor do you need to use the double bag method. Once your product is complete, freeze it for at least an hour and serve.

16. You will need:

- 1 cup of coconut cream
- 1 cup of plain yogurt
- ¾ cup of fresh spinach leaves
- ¼ cup of fresh mint leaves
- 6 tsps. of Truvia
- 1 tsp. of vanilla extract
- 1 tsp. of peppermint extract
- 1/2 cup of sugar free mini chocolate chips
- 1 disposable plastic storage container with lid

6. Information:

Prep time: 10 minutes

Total time: 1 hour

Serves: 6 (1/2 cup)

Calories per serving: 140

Total Calories: 840

Carbohydrates: 18

Information is based on regular plain yogurt. Your calories and carbs will vary slightly if you choose to substitute fat free or low-fat types.

16. Mint Chocolate Chip Ice Cream

Blend the spinach, and mint leaves with the coconut cream in a blender for 1 minute. Make sure the leaves are pureed down as much as possible. Add the rest of the ingredients except the chocolate chips.

Transfer the ice cream into your ice cream machine and churn for 30 minutes. Sprinkle the chocolate chips into the mixture. If you don't have a machine, transfer the mixture into a sealable container, and fold the the chips into the mixture with a spoon.

Set this in the freezer for an hour. Scoop and serve.

17. You will need:

- 1 cup of low fat cottage cheese
- 1/2 cups of unsweetened vanilla almond milk
- 2 tsps. of Truvia
- ¼ cup of cocoa powder
- 1 tbsp. of dark cooking chocolate
- 1 disposable plastic storage container with lid

17. Information:

Prep time: 20 minutes

Total time: 1 hour

Serves: 4 (1/2 cup)

Calories per serving: 100

Total Calories: 400

Carbohydrates: 11 g.

Information is based on low fat cottage cheese. Your calories and carbs will vary slightly if you choose to substitute fat free or low-fat types. Make sure to read the container and adjust based on the product you buy.

17. Grandma's Chocolate Ice Cream

An absolutely delishous recipe with the same consistency when using cream cheese. Substituting cream cheese for the cottage cheese will give your chocolate ice cream a more cheese cake flavor.

In one bowl add the vanilla, Truvia, cottage cheese, and almond milk. Stir in the cocoa powder and blend for one minute. Pour this into a sealable container and freeze for one hour. After the mixture is frozen churn it in your ice cream maker for 30 minutes, or continue processing it by using the double bag hame made method, as described in the previous recipes.

Chapter 4
Most Popular Flavors of Keto Frozen Treats

Here is an additional list of our most popular healthy frozen treats.

The following recipes can be made in a baking dish or bread loaf dish and rolled out with a spoon or ice cream scooper for a terrific serving.

Recipes (18 – 25)

18. Lemon Meringue Ice Cream
19. Low Carb Butter Pecan Ice Cream
20. Almond Frozen Yogurt
21. Coconut Chocolate Chip Frozen Yogurt
22. Peaches & Cream Ice Cream
23. Low Carb Key Lime Pie
24. Watermelon Ice Cream
25. Mermaid Ice Cream

18. You will need:

- 1 package of cream cheese
- ½ cup of half and half
- 1/2 cup of Truvia
- ½ cup of buttermilk
- 1 ½ tsp. vanilla bean paste
- 1/4 tsp. of slt
- 6 tbsps. of lemon curd
- 2 tbsps of sour cream
- 2 tsp. of lemon zest
- 1 tbsp. of lemon juice
- 1 disposable plastic storage container with lid
- Sugar free merangue cookies (optional)

18. Information:

Prep time: 20 minutes

Total time: 2 hours

Serves: 5 (1/2 cup)

Calories per serving: 300

Total Calories: 1,500

Carbohydrates: 18

18. Lemon Meringue Ice Cream

Combine the cream cheese, half and half, and Truvia, buttermilk, vanilla bean, and salt in a blender and set in the refrigerator to chill for a few hours.

Whisk together the lemon curd, sour cream, lemon juice, and lemon zest. Mix this until smooth. Blend this into the ice cream mixture.

Churn this in your ice cream machine for 30 minutes, and set into the freezer. If you do not use a machine, allow this to freeze using the two-bag freeze method as described in the previous recipe descriptions.

This flavor is popular when frozen between two cookies.

19. You will need:

- ½ cup of roasted pecans
- 1 ½ tbsps. of unsalted butter
- ¼ tsp. of salt
- ¼ cup of Truvia
- ¼ cup of Sukrin Gold
- 3 egg yolks
- 1 ½ cups of cream
- ½ cup of almond milk
- 1 tsp. of vanilla extract
- 1 disposable plastic storage container with lid

19. Information:

Prep time: 20 minutes

Total time: 1-3 hours

Serves: 5 (1/2 cup)

Calories per serving: 20

Total Calories: 1,000

Carbohydrates: 7 g.

Sukrin Gold is a natural alternative to brown sugar. It is almost a zero calorie, and zero carbohydrates from sugar alchohol. It is a derivitavle from corn starch and 100% natural.

19. Low Carb Butter Pecan Ice Cream

First, toast the pecans and soak in the butter and salt mix. In another bowl add the two sugar products. Add the egg youlks into the sugar. Over medium heat, bring the almond milk to a light simmer. Add the cream and then the sugar mixture. Bring this to 170 degrees for 3 minutes. Remove from heat and transfer to a sealable storage container. Freeze for 2 hours.

This recipe can be served right from the freezer after 6 hours, or you can churn it for another 30 minutes in your icecream maker for a smooth blend.

20. You will need:

- 1 can evaporated milk
- 2 cups of plain yogurt
- 1/4 cup of Truvia
- 1 tsp. of almond extract
- ¾ cup of crushed almonds
- 1 disposable plastic storage container with lid

20. Information:

Prep time: 10 minutes

Total time: 1-3 hours

Serves: 6 (1/2 cup)

Calories per serving: 150

Total Calories: 800

Carbohydrates: 16

Information is based on regular plain yogurt. Your calories and carbs will vary slightly if you choose to substitute fat free or low-fat types. Make sure to read the container and adjust based on the product you buy.

20. Almond Frozen Yogurt

Almond frozen yogurt is a top requested flavor. This recipe uses 1 can evaporated milk for a thick creamy texture. You can substitute vanilla flavored almond milk, but this will increase your sugar intake.

Blend all ingredients for 1 minute in the blender. This will mix the almonds into smaller pieces after they have been crushed.

Transfer into a disposable container and freeze for two hours. You can churn this recipe in your ice cream machine for 30 minutes for a smooth creamy texture. Frozen yogurt does not have to be churned if you want to skip this step.

Freeze well before serving.

21. You will need:

- 2 cups of whole milk
- 1 can of coconut milk
- 1 can evaporated milk
- ¼ cup of Truvia
- 1 tbsp. of lemon juice
- 3 tbsps. of coconut shavings
- ½ cup of sugar free chocolate chips
- 1 disposable plastic storage container with lid

21. Information:

Prep time: 2 minutes

Total time: 45 minutes

Serves: 6 (1/2 cup)

Calories per serving: 170

Total Calories: 1,020

Carbohydrates: 28

Sugar Free chocolate chips are not always readily abailable on your grocery store shelves. Substitute Hersheys sugar free chocolate syrup and swirl into the ice cream to make a fudge swirl.

21. Coconut Chocolate Chip Fozen Yogurt

Another simple recipe in high demand. Blend all the ingredients listed. If you want the coconut shavings to be finer than how they come in the package, blend into smaller pieces before adding to the mixture. Blend everything together except the chocolate chips.

Transfer this mixture into a sealable container and then pour the chips in and fold them into the mixture with a spoon.

Freeze for 6 hours, and serve.

22. You will need:

- 2 cans evaporated milk
- 1 ¼ cup whole milk
- ¼ cup Truvia
- 1 can of sliced peaches
- ¼ cup lemon juice
- ¼ tsp. salt
- 1 disposable plastic storage container with lid

22. Information:

Prep time: 20 minutes

Total time: 1-3 hours

Serves: 8 (1/2 cup)

Calories per serving: 240

Total Calories: 1840

Carbohydrates: 24

Fresh peaches are often preferred to canned peaches. If you choose to use sliced frech peaches, soak them for softness before adding to the mixture.

22. Peaches & Cream Ice Cream

In a large bowl mix the milk products, and set it aside in the refridgerater. Mix the peaches with sugar, lemon juice, and salt in a blender or food processor until smooth. Stir into milk mixture with the peach syrup from the can. (For less sugar, you canomit the syrup.)

If you choose to your ice cream machine pour milk mixture into freezer container of a 1-quart electric ice-cream maker, and freeze according to manufacturer's instructions.

Remove container with ice cream from ice-cream maker, and place in freezer for a few minutes. Transfer to an airtight container; freeze until firm, about 1 to 1 1/2 hours.

If you do not have an ice cream machine, place the ice cream contents in a plastic cooking bag and seal the bag. In another bag add 2 cups of ice cubes and ¼ tsp. salt. Place the first bag into the second bag. Seal the bag, and wrap a towel around the bag. Place in the freezer for 2 hours.

23. You will need:

- 2 cups heavy whipping cream
- 1 can of evaporated milk
- ¼ cup Truvia
- 1 tsp. vanilla
- green food coloring
- 3 tbsps. of lime juice
- 1 tsp lime zest
- ½ cup of sugar free white chocolate chips
- 1 disposable plastic storage container with lid

23. Information:

Prep time: 15 minutes

Total time: 1-2 hours

Serves: 10-12 (1/2 cup)

Calories per serving: 320

Total Calories: 3200

Carbohydrates: 12

If you have trouble finding sugar free chocolate chips. Look for Hershey's sugar free chocolate syrup. Drizzle it into the finished mixture and ceate a fudge swirl.

23. Low Carb Key Lime Pie

It only takes a hand mixer, a couple of bowls, and three ingredients to make.

This recipe takes just 3 ingredients folded into one another to make an easy, creamy, homemade vanilla ice cream that's ready to lick in just a few hours.

In another large bowl, whisk the vanilla into the sweetened condensed milk. Gently fold in the whipped cream with a spatula, slowly incorporating the two mixtures together so it stays light and aerated.

If making individual flavors, scoop the cream mixture into smaller bowls and gently fold in your desired mix-ins, or if making just one flavor, mix the ingredients directly into the cream mixture.

Transfer the mixture to an insulated tub or paper containers and freeze for 4-6 hours.

24. You will need:

- 4 cups of cubed watermelon
- 4 cups of whole milk
- 4 tsps. of Truvia
- ¼ tsp. of pure vanilla extract
- 1 disposable plastic storage container with lid

24. Information:

Prep time: 2 minutes

Total time: 45 minutes

Serves: 8 (1/2 cup)

Calories per serving: 220

Total Calories: 1760

Carbohydrates: 19

24. Watermelon Ice Cream

Watermelon Ice Cream is a fun summer flavor. This recipe is light and sweet and still offers a creamy rich flavor.

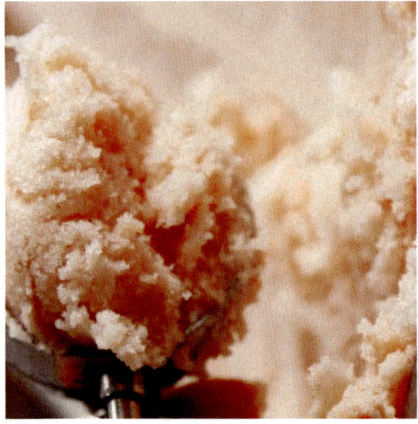

Mix all the ingredients in a blender. This recipe will freeze into a frosty treat without the help of the ice cream maker. However, if you want a rick smooth texture, churn it in your ice cream machine for 30 minutes.

25. You will need:

- 3 cups of heavy cream
- 1 can evaporated milk
- ¼ cup. of Truvia
- 1 tsp. pure vanilla extract
- Green, blue, purple food coloring
- 1 disposable plastic storage container with lid

25. Information:

Prep time: 10 minutes

Total time: 2 hours

Serves: 6 (1/2 cup)

Calories per serving: 170

Total Calories: 1,020

Carbohydrates: 28

Information is based on regular plain yogurt. Your calories and carbs will vary slightly if you choose to substitute fat free or low-fat types. Make sure to read the container and adjust based on the product you buy.

25. Mermaid Ice Cream

Do you want a fun ice cream, low in sugar, and full of colorful fun that the kids will love? Mermaid ice cream is vanilla flavored with a color explosion. For picky kids, this will be a sure-fire flavor that will make everyone happy.

Mix all the ingredients in the blender. Separate the mixture into five parts and add 3 drops of blue, green, and purple food coloring to each part. Leave two parts uncolored. Combine the two uncolored parts into a sealable container. Pour the colored parts into the mixture. Use a spoon or knife to swirl the colors. Top with sprinkles. Cover and freeze for 5 hours.

Remove form the freezer. Let the ice cream soften for 5 to 10 minutes. Scoop, and serve.

Additional Notes about Recipes

These recipes aren't limited to the ingredients listed. If you are carb conscious, or in need to limit your sugar you can substitute low sugar, fat free, or low carb products. If that sounds like a buzz kill to your palate, try these substitutes with a few table spoons of Truvia. Only 5 calories per tsp.

One note about artificial sweeteners and chemicals:

Many people simply refuse to add artificial sweeteners in their recipes because of the chemical additives. Splenda is popular among the Aktins followers, but some people claim they are wary due to the lack of thorough safety testing.

In this book, we recommend Truvia for all sugar substitute recipes. Truvia is the only sugar alternative offered at the coffee stand at Whole Foods grocery stores. When ordering a beverge from this natural food grocery chain, your choices are sugar or Truvia, that's it. When asked about the sugar options, one manager said, "these are the only ones that are natural, so it's what we offer."

Truvia - Truvia is a bit sweeter to the taste than raw sugar. One and ½ tsp. of Truvia is equal to One Tbsp. of sugar. ½ cup of Truvia is equal to 1 cup of raw sugar. It is made with three ingredients Erythritol, Sugar, and Stevia Leaf Extract.

Notice that we recommend you use disposable plastic containers with a lid when makng your frozen treats.

Milk – Not all milks are the same and not in the way you may think. Just because you choose a low-fat milk or skim milk it does not mean there will be fewer carbs. Substituting nut based milks like soy milk will not necessarily cut down on your carbohydrate intake. Because carbs are similar in different variations of milk, we recommend using regular whole milk because this will create a final product that is closest to the commercial brands that most people already recognize and enjoy.

Machine Free – In our directions we describe how to make these recipes without an ice crem machine. This is a standard method for all true ice ceam products, and those that are not ice cream can usually be placed in the freezer to set. If you do have a machine, you can use these recipes and make tham as you would normally use your ice cream macine. The processes to make ice cream ae similar. The machine will make your icecream consistant all the way through while the bag and towel method will give you a type of old fashioned ice cream.

Free Bonus Recipes (25 – 30)

26. Cake Pops

27. Ice Cream Cake Pops

28.

29.

30.

You will need:

- 1 and 1/4 cup of Truvia for baking
- 1 package of cream cheese
- 4 large egg yolks
- 3 cups of 2% milk
- 1 cup of half and half
- 3 cups of fresh blueberries
- ¼ cup of water
- 2 plastic cooking bags
- 2 tbsp of salt
- Ice cubes
- a towel

Information:

Prep time: 2 minutes

Total time: 45 minutes

Serves: 6 (1/2 cup)

Calories per serving: 170

Total Calories: 1,020

Carbohydrates: 28

Information is based on regular plain yogurt. Your calories and carbs will vary slightly if you choose to substitute fat free or low-fat types. Make sure to read the container and adjust based on the product you buy.

25: Cake Pops

Do you love a summer treat of blueberries and cream? We have our own low carb version in a blueberry cheese cake icecream.

Combine the egg yolks, sour cream, and 1 cup of Truvia in a large bowl with a beater. Combine the milk and half and half in a second bowl. Whisk half of the milk mixture to the cheese mixture while stirring constantly. Put the remaining half of the milk in the fridge.

Combine blueberries, ¼ cup of Truvia, and ¼ cup of water into the blender. Blend for one minute. Add the cheese mixture and blend for 1 minute.

Pour this mixture into a large plastic cooking bag and tie the top. Place this bag into a second bag filled with ice cubes and 2 tbsps. of salt. Wrap it in a towel and set this in the freezer for 1-3 hours. Continue checking until the ice cream is done.

You will need:

- 1 and 1/4 cup of Truvia for baking
- 1 package of cream cheese
- 4 large egg yolks
- 3 cups of 2% milk
- 1 cup of half and half
- 3 cups of fresh blueberries
- ¼ cup of water
- 2 plastic cooking bags
- 2 tbsp of salt
- Ice cubes
- a towel

Information:

Prep time: 2 minutes

Total time: 45 minutes

Serves: 6 (1/2 cup)

Calories per serving: 170

Total Calories: 1,020

Carbohydrates: 28

Information is based on regular plain yogurt. Your calories and carbs will vary slightly if you choose to substitute fat free or low-fat types. Make sure to read the container and adjust based on the product you buy.

26: Ice Cream Cake Pops

Do you love a summer treat of blueberries and cream? We have our own low carb version in a blueberry cheese cake icecream.

Combine the egg yolks, sour cream, and 1 cup of Truvia in a large bowl with a beater. Combine the milk and half and half in a second bowl. Whisk half of the milk mixture to the cheese mixture while stirring constantly. Put the remaining half of the milk in the fridge.

Combine blueberries, ¼ cup of Truvia, and ¼ cup of water into the blender. Blend for one minute. Add the cheese mixture and blend for 1 minute.

Pour this mixture into a large plastic cooking bag and tie the top. Place this bag into a second bag filled with ice cubes and 2 tbsps. of salt. Wrap it in a towel and set this in the freezer for 1-3 hours. Continue checking until the ice cream is done.

You will need:

- 1 and 1/4 cup of Truvia for baking
- 1 package of cream cheese
- 4 large egg yolks
- 3 cups of 2% milk
- 1 cup of half and half
- 3 cups of fresh blueberries
- ¼ cup of water
- 2 plastic cooking bags
- 2 tbsp of salt
- Ice cubes
- a towel

Information:

Prep time: 2 minutes

Total time: 45 minutes

Serves: 6 (1/2 cup)

Calories per serving: 170

Total Calories: 1,020

Carbohydrates: 28

Information is based on regular plain yogurt. Your calories and carbs will vary slightly if you choose to substitute fat free or low-fat types. Make sure to read the container and adjust based on the product you buy.

27: No Cook Blueberry Cheese Cake Ice Cream

Do you love a summer treat of blueberries and cream? We have our own w carb version in a blueberry cheese cake icecream.

Combine the egg yolks, sour cream, and 1 cup of Truvia in a large bowl with a beater. Combine the milk and half and half in a second bowl. Whisk half of the milk mixture to the cheese mixture while stirring constantly. Put the remaining half of the milk in the fridge.

Combine blueberries, ¼ cup of Truvia, and ¼ cup of water into the blender. Blend for one minute. Add the cheese mixture and blend for 1 minute.

Pour this mixture into a large plastic cooking bag and tie the top. Place this bag into a second bag filled with ice cubes and 2 tbsps. of salt. Wrap it in a towel and set this in the freezer for 1-3 hours. Continue checking until the ice cream is done.

You will need:

- 1 and 1/4 cup of Truvia for baking
- 1 package of cream cheese
- 4 large egg yolks
- 3 cups of 2% milk
- 1 cup of half and half
- 3 cups of fresh blueberries
- ¼ cup of water
- 2 plastic cooking bags
- 2 tbsp of salt
- Ice cubes
- a towel

Information:

Prep time: 2 minutes

Total time: 45 minutes

Serves: 6 (1/2 cup)

Calories per serving: 170

Total Calories: 1,020

Carbohydrates: 28

Information is based on regular plain yogurt. Your calories and carbs will vary slightly if you choose to substitute fat free or low-fat types. Make sure to read the container and adjust based on the product you buy.

28: No Cook Blueberry Cheese Cake Ice Cream

Do you love a summer treat of blueberries and cream? We have our own low carb version in a blueberry cheese cake icecream.

Combine the egg yolks, sour cream, and 1 cup of Truvia in a large bowl with a beater. Combine the milk and half and half in a second bowl. Whisk half of the milk mixture to the cheese mixture while stirring constantly. Put the remaining half of the milk in the fridge.

Combine blueberries, ¼ cup of Truvia, and ¼ cup of water into the blender. Blend for one minute. Add the cheese mixture and blend for 1 minute.

Pour this mixture into a large plastic cooking bag and tie the top. Place this bag into a second bag filled with ice cubes and 2 tbsps. of salt. Wrap it in a towel and set this in the freezer for 1-3 hours. Continue checking until the ice cream is done.

You will need:

- 1 and 1/4 cup of Truvia for baking
- 1 package of cream cheese
- 4 large egg yolks
- 3 cups of 2% milk
- 1 cup of half and half
- 3 cups of fresh blueberries
- ¼ cup of water
- 2 plastic cooking bags
- 2 tbsp of salt
- Ice cubes
- a towel

Information:

Prep time: 2 minutes

Total time: 45 minutes

Serves: 6 (1/2 cup)

Calories per serving: 170

Total Calories: 1,020

Carbohydrates: 28

Information is based on regular plain yogurt. Your calories and carbs will vary slightly if you choose to substitute fat free or low-fat types. Make sure to read the container and adjust based on the product you buy.

29: No Cook Blueberry Cheese Cake Ice Cream

Do you love a summer treat of blueberries and cream? We have our own low carb version in a blueberry cheese cake icecream.

Combine the egg yolks, sour cream, and 1 cup of Truvia in a large bowl with a beater. Combine the milk and half and half in a second bowl. Whisk half of the milk mixture to the cheese mixture while stirring constantly. Put the remaining half of the milk in the fridge.

Combine blueberries, ¼ cup of Truvia, and ¼ cup of water into the blender. Blend for one minute. Add the cheese mixture and blend for 1 minute.

Pour this mixture into a large plastic cooking bag and tie the top. Place this bag into a second bag filled with ice cubes and 2 tbsps. of salt. Wrap it in a towel and set this in the freezer for 1-3 hours. Continue checking until the ice cream is done.

Made in the USA
Las Vegas, NV
05 March 2025

19118630R00029